STABLEMATES
Vital Statistics
A Guide to Conformation

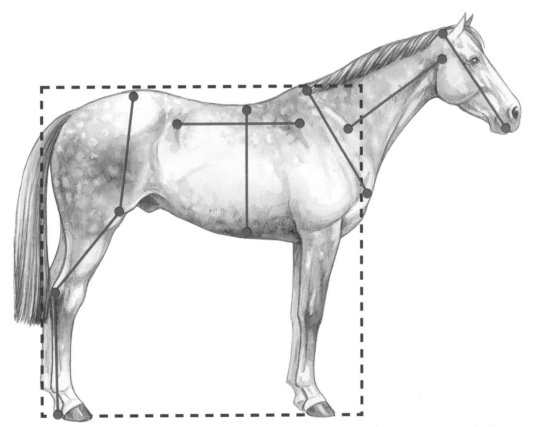

Written and Illustrated by
Maggie Raynor

First published in 2006 by
The Pony Club
Stoneleigh Park
Kenilworth
Warwickshire
CV8 2RW

Produced for the Pony Club by Barbara Cooper
Designed by Paul Harding

2 4 5 3 1

ISBN 0-9548863-0-5

British Library Cataloguing in Publication Data available on request.

Printed in China

Contents

Introduction

When we discuss a horse or pony's conformation we are referring to his general make and shape, and to the relative proportions of the various parts of his body: i.e. his 'vital statistics'.

In human terms, vital statistics are often thought of in the context of beauty contests where the shape and proportions of several bodies (usually female) are being judged, with first prize awarded to the one considered to be the most attractive. Beauty is the first and only consideration here; function – or the ability to do a hard day's work – is not on the agenda.

When assessing the conformation of a horse, things are very much the other way round: function must always be considered before beauty; in fact an animal whose basic structure is faulty is most unlikely to be thought attractive.

In the human body we have a limited concept of what is beautiful – not too tall or too short, not too fat or too thin. However, in equine terms a short-legged, sturdy cob can be just as attractive and have just as good a conformation as an elegant hack. Our assessment of a horse's framework is to a great extent based on the job he has to do, and these jobs are many and varied.

Originally our ancestors would have used the horse as a pack animal; later on in agriculture and as a riding or a war horse. Before railways and motor-cars arrived on the scene, the horse was the only means we had of getting ourselves and our worldly goods from A to B; he either pulled us along in carts and carriages or carried us on his back. To fill these various needs, horses with different body-shapes were specially bred: strong and sturdy for ploughing or heavy-hauling, lighter and faster for riding-horses or for those intended to impress one's neighbour when harnessed to an expensive carriage.

Today the horse is used mainly for sport or pleasure, but again his tasks are varied. He can be used for show jumping, racing, dressage, long-distance riding, eventing, gymkhanas, polo, showing and driving – or he can be just a good all-round pony who excels at nothing but being your best friend.

Although the body-shape of the various horses will differ according to breed and discipline, there are basic structural principles which apply to every horse if he is to work for any length of time without discomfort or physical damage. Becoming familiar with these principles will not only enable you to assess the soundness and performance-potential of any horse or pony you are thinking of buying; it will also help you to understand and work with the physical limitations of each and every horse that you ride.

Looking at the Whole Picture

Assessing the conformation of a horse can be compared to looking at a painting in a gallery. Before getting involved in the finer details, you stand back and give yourself time to take in the whole picture.

Similarly, when examining a horse or pony, the first step is to let your eye run over his whole body, from the side, behind and from the front. By doing this you are able to check that his balance, proportions and outlines are correct before going on to examine the various parts of his body in greater detail.

Balance

Good balance. Cob

Good balance. Thoroughbred

In terms of conformation, balance means that all the elements of the horse's body should fit together to make a pleasing and harmonious whole. The body of a Shire horse can be just as balanced as that of a Thoroughbred, but if you can imagine the front end of one attached to the back end of the other – there all harmony ends! Fortunately things are never as bad as this, but in your preliminary examination of the horse you should be looking for any part of his body which seems out of proportion to the rest. Is the head too big or too small for the body? Does the neck look too long or too short, too chunky or too thin? Does the size and shape of the hind quarters match the size and shape of the forehand? Although such departures from perfect balance may not cause actual unsoundness, extra stress will be placed on the structure as a whole if one part is out of proportion to the rest.

Balance between the forehand and the quarters is particularly important. The hind quarters are the horse's engine, equipped with large muscles which propel him both forwards and upwards. The forehand acts to a great extent as a shock-absorber; it takes the impact as the forelegs hit the ground after each stride, or on landing after a jump.

A horse with small hind quarters will be lacking in power and tend to go on the forehand, pulling himself along by his stronger front legs rather than pushing from behind. The horse with a weak forehand will have an uncomfortable jolting stride, and his rider will feel insecure due to there being so little of the horse's body in front of the saddle to balance the power coming from behind.

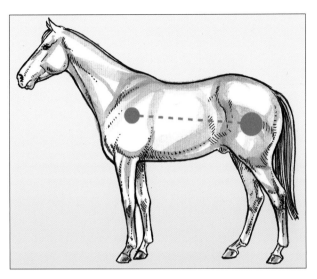

Weak forehand. The horse is heavy behind.

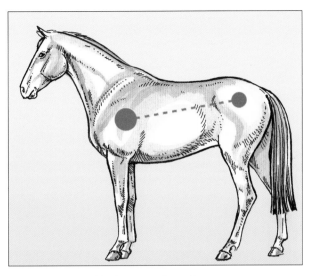

Weak quarters. The horse is front-heavy.

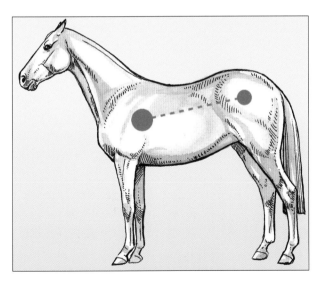

Croup high. Weight is on the forehand.

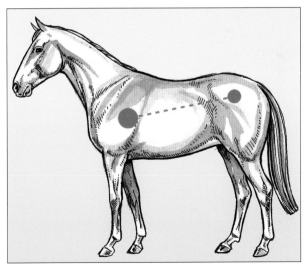

Large head. Weight is on the forehand.

Proportion

Although no two horses are exactly alike, and ideal proportions may vary slightly from breed to breed, there are ways of checking that the proportions of the individual horse that you are examining are more or less correct.

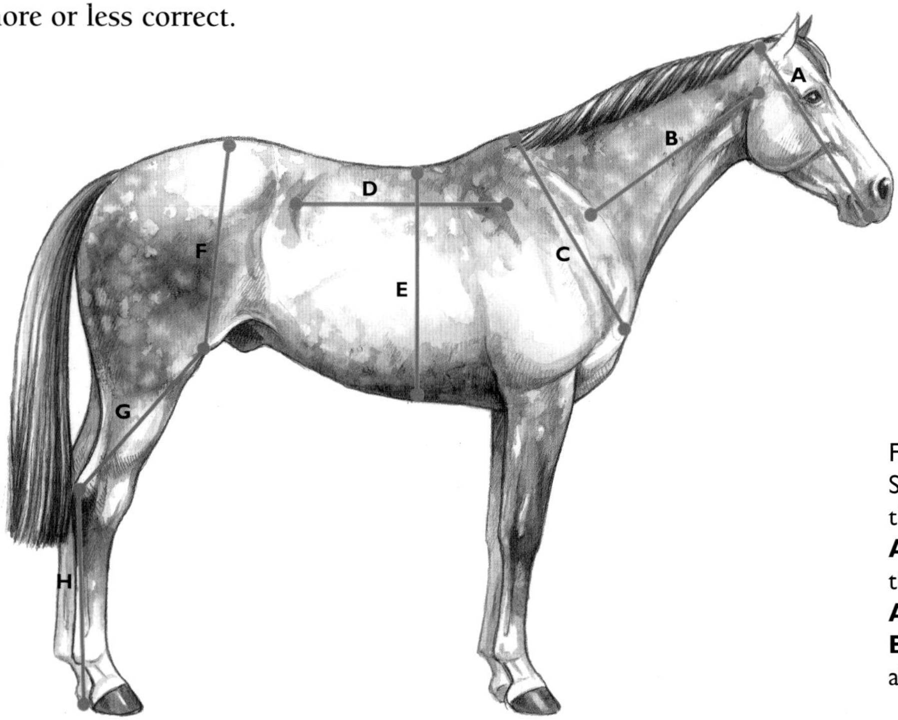

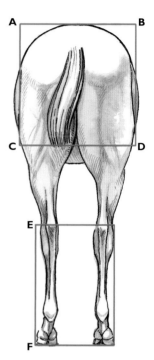

Fig. 2
Seen from behind the ideal proportions of the hind quarters should fit into a square.
AC/BD The height from the croup to the thighs is equal to:
AB/CD The width across the thighs,
EF The height from hoof to hock should also measure the same as **AC/AB**.

Fig. 1
The length of the head (line **A**) should equal approximately:
B the length of the neck from the wing of the atlas to the shoulder muscles,
C the length of the shoulder from the apex of the withers to the point of the shoulder,
D the length of the body from the edge of the scapula to the last rib,
E the depth of the girth,

F from the croup to the patella,
G from the stifle to the point of the hock,
H from the point of the hock to the ground.

These measurements should help you to establish if the size of the head is correct, and also if the various other parts of the body are in correct proportion to each other.

Fig. 3
The length of the horse's body (line **A** – **B**) should be the same as the height from withers to hoof (line **C** – **D**). In other words the body of the horse should fit nicely into a square. Remembering this will help you to check if the horse's back is too long or too short.

Fig. 4
A pony's proportions are different from those of a horse; his legs are shorter in relation to his body.

The length of the body (**A** – **B** is greater than the height (**C** – **D**).
The length of the legs (**D** – **E**) is roughly the same as the depth through the girth (**E** – **C**).

Symmetry

Asymmetrical shapes   Symmetrical shapes

An object which is symmetrical is capable of being divided into two identical halves when cut down the middle. Few human beings, or horses, have a perfectly symmetrical body. We all have one side which is more dominant than the other; if we are right-handed our right side is dominant, if we are left-handed then it is the left. The muscles on the dominant side become more developed, as they are used more than those on the weaker side. Horses are usually able to bend more easily to one side than the other; a young unschooled horse will prefer to strike off with one particular leg leading at canter regardless of whether he is cantering left or right. This one-sidedness is normal, and although any stiffness in one rein will be easily felt by the rider, the resulting unequal muscle development may not be visible to an observer on the ground. The neck may be more developed on one side than the other, or maybe the horse has a slight bend through his body – but these discrepancies are minor and can be improved by knowledgeable riding.

More serious irregularities are relevant because they weaken the structure as a whole. If weight and stress cannot be distributed equally throughout the body, damage will be done to those areas which are forced to bear more than their share, resulting in poor performance or even lameness.

Ideally, the horse's body should look the same on both right and left sides. This should be checked by observing the horse:
• from directly in front,
• from directly behind,
• from behind and slightly above (standing on a chair if this can be done safely),
• from either side.

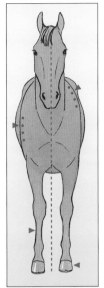
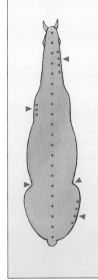

Standing in front of the horse allows you to check that both shoulders are equally muscled, with no areas which are wasted or underdeveloped. Both legs should look straight, with the toes pointing forwards.

From behind you are checking not only for equal muscle development in the quarters, but also that the bones of the pelvis are in alignment. The bones at the point of croup should be level, as should both hips. The tail should hang vertically and not be carried over to one side. These points should be checked very carefully, as any lack of symmetry in this region could indicate that there has been displacement of the pelvis. Both hind legs should appear straight, with no excessive turning in or out of the hock.

When examining the horse from above you are looking for equal development of the muscles on either side of the neck, back and pelvis; for any irregularities in the path of the spinal vertebrae; and for a straight line from the horse's front to his back (hind quarters in alignment with the forehand).

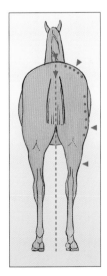
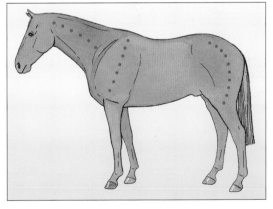

From the side you are again looking for equal muscle development, although this is difficult as there is no way of seeing both sides at once for comparison.

There are many reasons for asymmetry (or irregularity) in the horse's body; bad riding, shoeing, ill-fitting tack, falls and injury, as well as faulty conformation, can cause unequal muscle development or even displacement of the skeleton. In many cases these irregularities will improve if corrective measures are taken – but, if in doubt, a vet's opinion should be sought.

AREAS OF ASYMMETRY

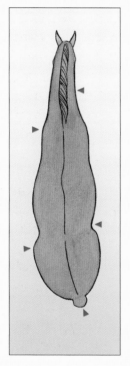

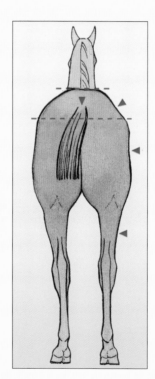

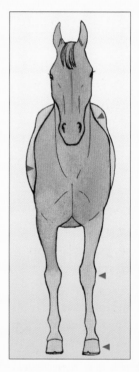

- Muscle wastage on neck and shoulders.
- Kinks in the spine.
- Unlevel hips.
- Quarters not aligned with the forehand.

- Tilting of the pelvis.
- Tail held to one side.
- Muscle wastage on quarters.

- Muscle wastage on the shoulders.
- Forelegs not straight.
- Toe turned inwards.

Examining the Structure

The skeleton is the framework of the horse's body. It is the skeleton's proportions which determine whether a horse has good or bad conformation. Once a bone is fully developed it can only change in a limited way – for example, new areas of bone can be laid down to repair an injury, or the bone can thicken as the result of exercise. A horse with established conformational defects – such as a large head or a short neck – will always have them; they cannot be put right by feeding or exercise. The muscles, however, will develop and increase in size if the horse is given proper exercise and nutrition.

When making your first overall assessment of a horse, his age and condition should be taken into account. If he is young, unfit or underfed the muscles will not be fully developed and the horse may look thin, or even poor. On the other hand, his basic structure will be easily visible and if his proportions and limbs are correct, there is every chance that with proper feeding and exercise he will develop into a sound and good-looking animal. Bear in mind that a young horse often grows in fits and starts. The hind quarters will occasionally overtake the front, making him croup high. By the age of four the withers will usually have caught up with the quarters; but an adult horse who is croup high will remain so for the rest of his life.

If the horse or pony is grossly overweight, remember that excess body-fat can cover the structure to such an extent that minor flaws in the neck, shoulders and quarters can be hidden – which may be why so many animals in the show-ring are over weight!

The neck, shoulders and hind quarters are areas of the body where major muscle groups are situated, so these are the parts which will show the most development and improvement in a young or unfit horse. A few weeks of consistent work can make quite a difference to the appearance of such an animal.

In a horse with good conformation the top line should consist of a series of gentle curves: one blending smoothly into another without any sharp angles or dips. Standing back from the horse gives you the best opportunity to check the top line. The neck should not dip just in front of the withers and bulge out on the underside (known as 'ewe' neck). The withers should not be too flat or too prominent. The back should not be dipped ('sway' back) or arch up just before the croup ('roach' back). The hind quarters should slope gently down from the croup to the tail, but not at too oblique an angle ('goose' rump) or too flat. The croup should not be higher than the quarters ('croup high'). The tail should be well set onto the hind quarters, level with the back and carried away from the body, not set low and tucked into the quarters.

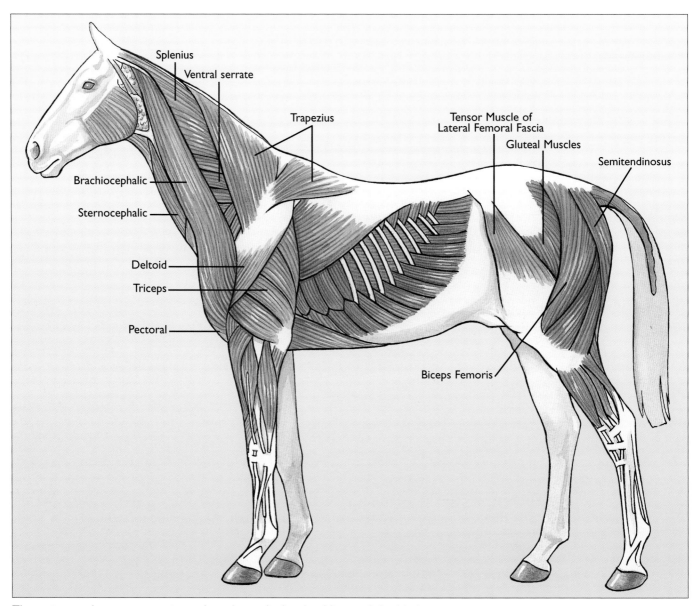

The main muscle-masses are situated on the neck, the shoulders and the hind quarters.
These are the parts of the body that will develop with feeding and exercise.

THE SKELETON

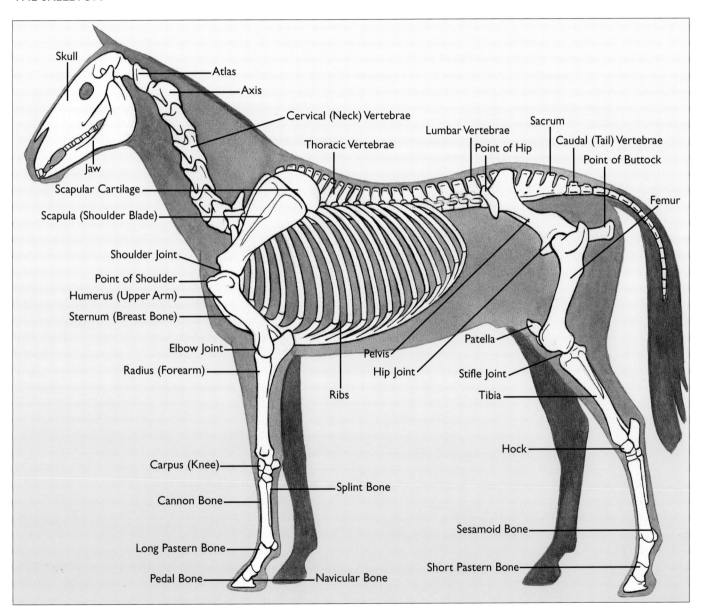

Skull

Atlas

Axis

Cervical (Neck) Vertebrae

Thoracic Vertebrae

Lumbar Vertebrae

Sacrum

Point of Hip

Caudal (Tail) Vertebrae

Point of Buttock

Jaw

Scapular Cartilage

Scapula (Shoulder Blade)

Femur

Shoulder Joint

Point of Shoulder

Humerus (Upper Arm)

Sternum (Breast Bone)

Elbow Joint

Radius (Forearm)

Pelvis

Hip Joint

Ribs

Patella

Stifle Joint

Tibia

Hock

Carpus (Knee)

Splint Bone

Cannon Bone

Long Pastern Bone

Pedal Bone

Navicular Bone

Sesamoid Bone

Short Pastern Bone

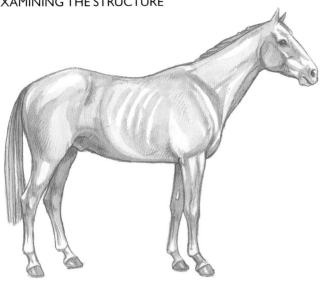

A poor - or thin - horse with a correct frame.
Given correct feeding and exercise he will develop
into a good, sound horse.

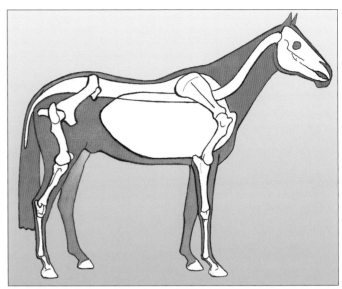

The skeleton of a horse with a correct frame.

A poor horse who has an incorrect frame.

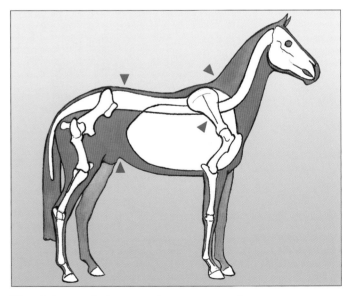

The skeleton of a horse with an incorrect frame.
He has a roach back and a straight shoulder.
He is also ewe-necked and herring-gutted.
These are skeletal problems which cannot be improved.

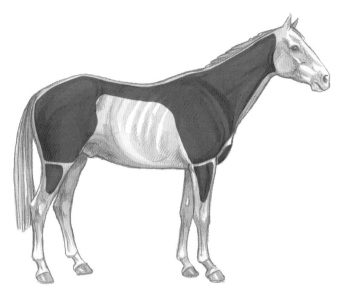

BEFORE - an unfit horse, showing the muscles that will develop with work.

AFTER - the same horse after muscle development.

Mature horse with croup-high conformation.
This is a skeletal problem which cannot be corrected.

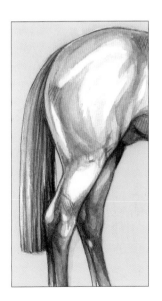

Correctly placed tail.

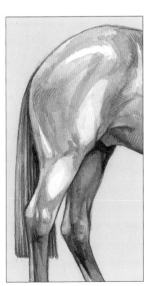

Low-set tail.

The Top Line

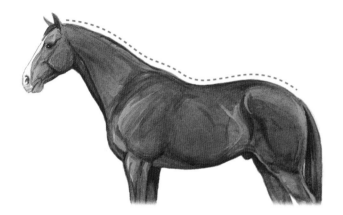

A horse with a correct top line: a series of gentle curves running smoothly into each other.

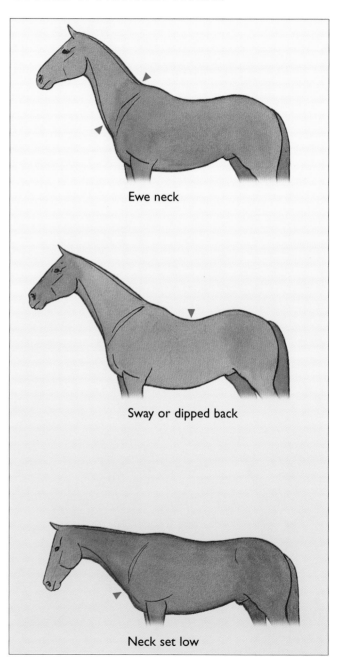

Ewe neck

Sway or dipped back

Neck set low

The top line can be improved by correct schooling, as long as there are no skeletal faults. The neck, back and quarter muscles will develop with exercise, giving a more rounded and attractive appearance to the top line.

High wither

Low wither

Roach back

Goose rump

Croup high

Flat croup

Looking at the Detail

Having taken time to assess the horse from a distance, where any short-comings in proportion, balance and symmetry should have been noted, we can then go on to examine the various parts of the body in greater detail.

The Points of the Horse

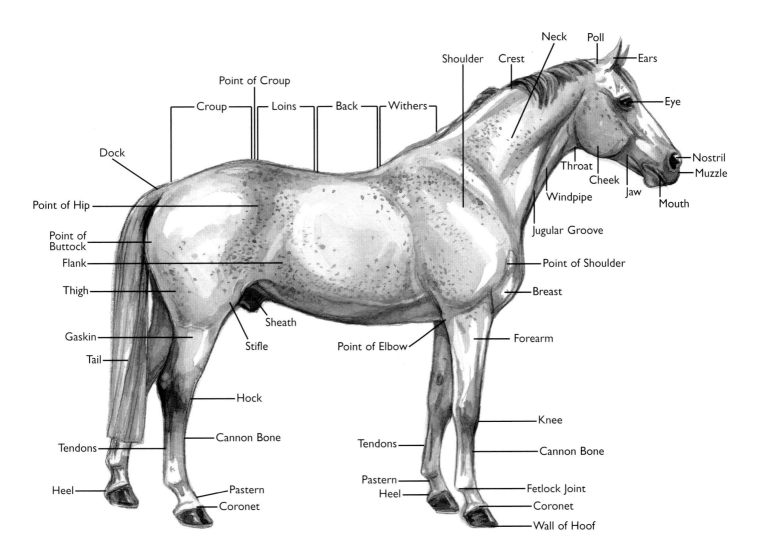

Point of Croup

Croup — Loins — Back — Withers

Shoulder — Crest — Neck — Poll — Ears

Eye

Dock

Nostril

Muzzle

Throat

Cheek — Jaw — Mouth

Point of Hip

Windpipe

Jugular Groove

Point of
Buttock

Point of Shoulder

Flank

Breast

Thigh

Sheath

Gaskin

Stifle

Point of Elbow — Forearm

Tail

Hock

Knee

Tendons

Cannon Bone

Tendons — Cannon Bone

Heel

Pastern

Pastern

Fetlock Joint

Coronet

Heel — Coronet

Wall of Hoof

The Head

The head is the most expressive part of the horse's body. As with humans, we tend to assess a horse's personality by his facial characteristics. A large eye denotes kindness and intelligence, and a small eye meanness; a bump between the eyes can indicate stubbornness; large ears a generous nature, and so on. Most of these characteristics are only relevant in the show ring where the horse is being judged as much on type and charm as on structural soundness; it is far safer to base your assessment of a horse's character and temperament on his reaction to being handled and ridden.

More important to consider are those aspects of the head which relate to function and overall balance – the first of these being proportion. The size of the head should be in keeping with the rest of the body. As the skull is heavy, being composed of relatively dense bony structures, a large head will affect the balance of the whole body, weighing the horse down on the forehand. If the head is heavy it should be coupled with a short and well-muscled neck: this being structurally stronger than one which is long and thin. A small head attached to a short neck will limit the horse's ability to balance himself, making him more likely to fall if he slips or lands badly after jumping.

The head of a Shire horse with a Roman nose.

The dished face of an Arabian horse.

A heavy jawbone, set too closely into the neck. This horse would find flexion from the poll uncomfortable, as his jawbone compresses the salivary glands.

A narrow head with eyes set to the front; small nostrils and large ears.

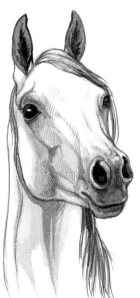

A correctly-shaped jaw, well set on to the neck. There is enough room at the throat to allow the head to flex without interfering with the parotid glands.

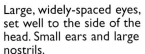

Large, widely-spaced eyes, set well to the side of the head. Small ears and large nostrils.

A long, narrow head with lop ears. The eyes are small, and there is a bump between them.

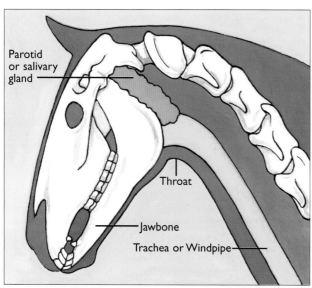

A correctly-shaped jaw does not interfere with the parotid glands when the head is flexed.

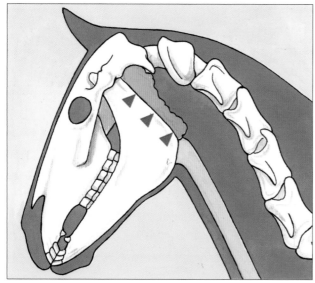

A heavy, sharply angled jaw can constrict the parotid glands, making flexion uncomfortable.

The shape of the nose varies according to breed. Many heavy horses and those of Spanish or Barb descent have a Roman nose, where the bones at the front of the face curve outwards. The Arabian horse has the opposite structure – a dished face which curves inwards. Neither shape is correct or incorrect; the horse's head should be in keeping with its breed or type.

The horse obtains his supply of oxygen through the nostrils: therefore large, open nostrils enabling maximum intake of air will be an advantage – especially for a horse expected to perform at speed.

According to showing conventions, the eyes should be large and 'well set apart' – but how do these characteristics affect the horse's ability to see? A large eye may well give a greater field of vision than a small one. Eyes set well apart will be situated more towards the side of the face than those which are not separated to such an extent by the width of the forehead. The further the horse's eye is situated to the side of his head the better will be his peripheral vision (the distance the horse can see to the side and to the rear). This is a definite advantage to a prey animal grazing with its head down, but is not so helpful to a horse being ridden into a large jump at speed! A narrow head, although it may not look so attractive, may in fact give advantage to a jumping horse by slightly increasing his field of forward vision.

Although the shape and size of the horse's ears have no bearing on performance, they do affect his expression – and many people believe that his

The two branches of the jawbone should be set well apart. This will allow the tongue to lie comfortably in the tongue groove, and the passage of air through the trachea will not be restricted.

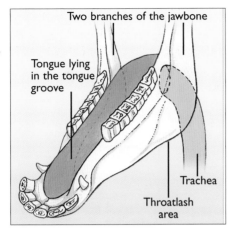

Two branches of the jawbone

Tongue lying in the tongue groove

Trachea

Throatlash area

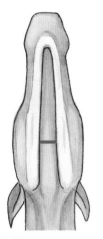

Narrow jaws

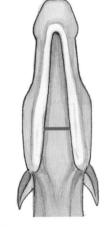

Correctly-spaced jaws

The structure of the horse's jaw and the set of the jawbone onto the neck should be carefully examined and considered. The jawbone attaches to the skull just behind the ears, in an area which also accommodates the parotid (or salivary) glands. If the horse has a heavy jawbone, coupled closely to a short, thick neck, he will not be able to flex his head at the poll without the salivary glands becoming compressed by the angle of the jaw. This will cause discomfort, and discourage him from working in the correct outline. There should be plenty of space between the jawbone and the neck to allow the horse to flex comfortably; the angle of the jaw should be softly rounded for the same reason. Any tension in the jaw will be passed on through the rest of the body; a horse which has poor jaw conformation will never achieve a happy and relaxed way of going – and neither will his rider!

The lower jawbone is divided into two branches, along which runs the tongue and between which (at the neck end) lies the trachea, or windpipe. The distance between these two branches is relevant: if they are too close together the tongue-groove may be too narrow to accommodate the tongue, which will give bitting problems. The windpipe is also likely to be compressed when the horse flexes his head, causing problems with breathing. Jawbones which are well spaced at the throatlash area are ideal; you can check this distance by placing your fist between the jawbones at their widest point; there should be room enough to allow you to do this.

temperament can be revealed by them. The ears can be large or small, sharply pricked, curly or lopped (carried out to the side and drooping downward). For showing purposes the ears should be in keeping with the type and character of the head – small and pricked for a pony, larger for a horse or cob, curly and expressive for an Arab.

The Neck

The neck and head are crucial to the horse's agility and sense of balance; an analysis of the movement of a horse jumping at liberty will reveal to what extent this is so… On approaching the jump the horse lifts his neck and raises his head. On take-off his neck is still raised but his nose is tucked in. Over the jump he stretches his neck down and out, and drops his nose. On landing he lifts his neck and stretches out his head. For his recovery stride and get-away he once again stretches out his neck and drops his nose…all in all a very complex procedure.

If you look at the drawings on pages 14 and 15 – the muscles and skeleton – you will see that the neck is composed mainly of muscle, supported only by the cervical vertebrae. If the conformation of the skeleton is correct, the shape of the neck can be greatly improved by building up the muscle through exercise. There are, however, several conformational problems which cannot be overcome.

A neck which looks upside-down is known as a 'ewe' neck: the top line is concave (hollow) instead of being convex (rounded); the neck dips just before the withers and bulges out on the underside. A horse with this conformation will not be able to flex his jaw, round his neck and lift his back; neither will he be able to engage his hocks underneath his body or work in a correct outline. He can be helped to some extent by corrective schooling. Working long and low to stretch and loosen the neck will improve his way of going, but as the problem is one of faulty structure it cannot be completely resolved.

A 'swan' neck is similar to the 'ewe' neck, but is further complicated by an extra bend at the top of the neck near the poll. This may look attractive to the unknowledgeable; however, the horse will not only have all the problems associated with a ewe neck but additionally he will find it all too easy to tuck his chin into his neck and thus be able to evade the action of the bit.

HOW THE HORSE USES HIS HEAD AND NECK WHEN JUMPING

APPROACH
Head and neck lifted to see the jump.

TAKE-OFF
Neck raised and nose tucked in.

OVER THE JUMP
Neck stretched out and down, nose dropped.

Horse with correct neck conformation

A 'bull' neck is a short, stocky neck which is thick through the gullet. Horses with this problem find it impossible to flex through the head and jaw, and can feel very heavy in the hand as a result.

If the neck is set very low into the shoulders the horse will be unbalanced through extra weight falling onto his forehand. It will be difficult to lighten the forehand by elevation of the head and neck, which is a requirement of more advanced schooling.

INCORRECT NECK CONFORMATION

Head coming low out of the shoulder

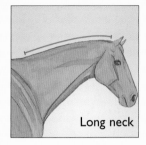

Long neck

Ewe neck

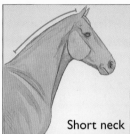

Short neck

Swan neck

Bull neck

LANDING
Neck lifted and head stretched out.

RECOVERY
Neck stretched out, nose dropped.

GET-AWAY
Neck stretched out, nose dropped.

The Withers

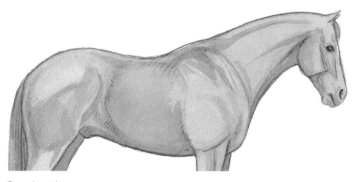

Good withers

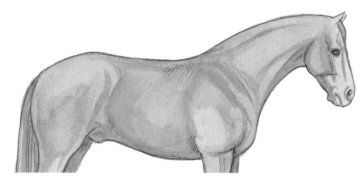

Low withers

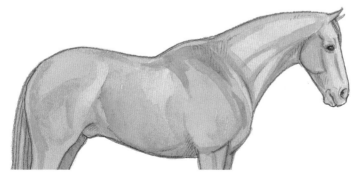

High Withers

The withers are formed by the dorsal spinous processes of the first ten thoracic vertebrae, to which are attached various muscles and ligaments. In a horse with good conformation the withers are neither too flat nor too pronounced but should be long and well-defined, blending smoothly into both the neck and back. Bad conformation of the withers will generally not affect the soundness or performance of the horse, but will give problems with the fit of the saddle.

If the withers are flat there is nothing to stabilise the saddle, which will slip to the side. If withers are too high it will be difficult to fit the saddle so that it clears the withers at the pommel and does not pinch the muscles on either side.

The Chest

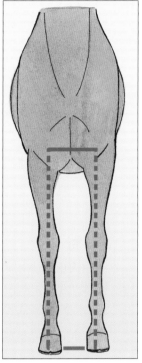

Correct conformation

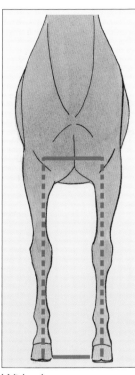

Wide chest

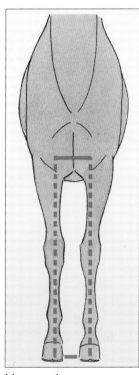

Narrow chest

Seen from the front, the ideal chest is deep enough to accommodate a good set of heart and lungs without being too wide or too narrow.

If the chest is narrow the forelegs will be set too close together, which may result in faulty movement, with one hoof striking into and cutting the opposite leg. The horse may also be 'base-wide' (see 'forelegs'), and due to poor lung capacity he may be lacking in stamina. If the chest is narrow as the result of inadequate feeding and exercise this may be corrected by adjusting the feed and exercise levels, as there is no fixed skeletal connection between the forelegs and the ribcage.

A horse with a wide chest may move with a rolling gait, and have his forelegs set too far underneath him. Often, horses with this conformation are 'base-narrow' (see 'forelegs'). However, a broad chest is very strong and can give the horse good stability.

The Forelegs

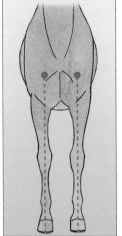
Correct conformation

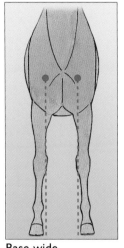
Base wide

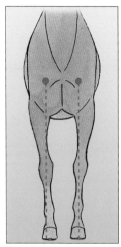
Base narrow

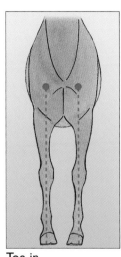
Toe in

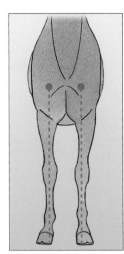
Toe out

To be structurally sound the foreleg should appear vertical from both the front and the side. From the front, a line dropped vertically from the point of the shoulder should pass through the centre of the knee, cannon bone, fetlock, pastern and foot. If this is so, the column of bones which make up the leg will be in perfect alignment, and the stresses of weight and concussion will be transmitted directly along the length of the leg without putting any one area of the structure under extra pressure. If any part of the leg is out of alignment, the conformation is considered faulty.

Seen from the side, a line dropped vertically from the elbow joint (not the point of the elbow) should pass through the centre of the knee and fetlock joints, meeting the ground just behind the bulbs of the heels. Again, any deviation from the vertical is a fault in conformation which will put unequal stresses on the structure of the leg.

Other points to be considered when assessing the forelegs are:

- The forearm should be well muscled.
- The cannon bones should be short and strong with a good width of bone under the knee.
- The tendons should be hard, strong and well defined.
- The knees should be large and flat.
- The knee and fetlock joints should be clean and hard, with no swelling or puffiness.
- The pasterns should ideally slope at 45°. Short, upright pasterns will not act well as shock absorbers. Long sloping pasterns will be weak and prone to injury.

FORELEGS

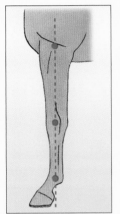

Correct conformation

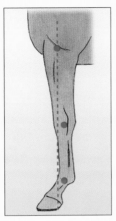

Camped under

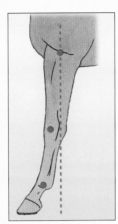

Camped out

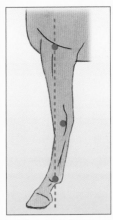

Back at the knee

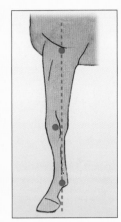

Over at the knee

PASTERNS

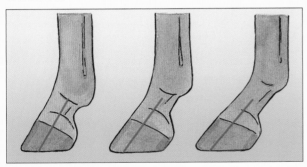

Upright pasterns

Correct pastern conformation

Weak, sloping pasterns

FAULTS IN THE FORELEG

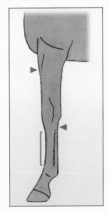

Weak forearm: tied-in below the knee, long cannon bones

Damaged tendons

Puffy joints

The Barrel

The barrel – or that portion of the horse's body between withers and hips – is the container for the heart, lungs and various other internal organs. The heart and lungs fuel the body tissues with oxygen; they need plenty of room to do their job properly. A barrel with good conformation will provide this space; a barrel with bad conformation will limit it.

The rib-cage gives the barrel its shape; it surrounds and protects the heart and lungs, and is also actively involved in the process of breathing. As the ribs expand they enable the lungs to fill with air, and as they contract, the air is expelled. Well-rounded ribs will give maximum room to the heart and lungs; such ribs are termed 'well sprung'.

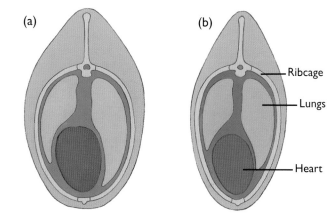

Cross-section through the barrel:
(a) Good conformation - plenty of space for heart and lungs;
(b) Slab-sided conformation - heart and lung space restricted by the ribcage.

A horse with good barrel conformation

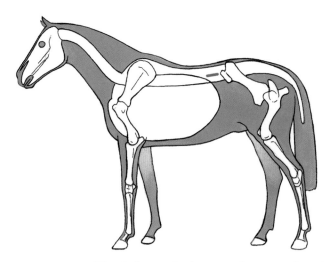

The skeleton of a horse with correct barrel conformation, showing a hand's width between the last rib and the point of hip.

The rib-cage should extend well back towards the hip, ideally allowing a hand's width between the last rib and the point of hip. A horse with this conformation is said to be 'well ribbed up'. A horse with too great a distance between rib and hip is known as 'herring-gutted'. The underside of a herring-gutted horse will not run in a gentle curve from front to back as it should, but will slope noticeably upwards towards the stifle. There are strong abdominal muscles located in this region of the body which affect the horse's ability to lift his back and engage his quarters; this plus the fact that herring-gutted horses tend to be long in the back will make such a horse weaker than one of good conformation.

This horse is long in the back and very shallow through the girth. His heart and lung room is restricted.

The conformation of the rib-cage is important from the rider's point of view because this is the part of the horse that we sit on. The rib-cage supports both the saddle and the rider, and is the point of contact between the rider's legs and the horse. A slab-sided horse (one with flat, badly sprung ribs) will be an uncomfortable ride not only because there is so little of him but also due to the fact that the saddle may not be stable. Such horses will often be lacking in heart and lung capacity, although if the rib-cage is deep this will compensate for the lack of width.

A herring-gutted horse

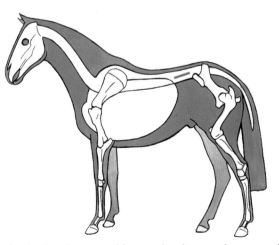

In the herring-gutted horse, the distance between the last rib and the point of the hip is greater than a hand's width.

The Back

The horse's back extends from his withers to his hips. The ideal back is of medium length, gently curved on the top line and sufficiently well-muscled to carry both saddle and rider with comfort.

The proportions of the back are related to both soundness and performance. The back is the bridge between forehand and quarters, but whereas most bridges run in a straight line between their two anchor-points, the horse's back curves slightly downwards. This concave profile weakens the structure of the back – and to make matters worse the rider adds his or her weight to the problem!

A short back, although strong, could be lacking in suppleness, give a jarring ride, and make the horse more likely to overreach (the toes of the hind feet treading on the heels of the front feet). An over-long back may be more supple than a short one, but it will be structurally weaker and the horse will have difficulty achieving collection.

Many people prefer a horse to be 'short-coupled' – meaning that his back is slightly on the short side – as this gives strength and enables the horse to carry weight without risk of strain or injury.

A 'sway' back, or one that dips more than it should in the middle, can cause difficulties for both horse and rider. The weight of the rider pressing down on this already bowed structure could give the horse discomfort, added to by the fact that the saddle will not fit correctly. Because of the dip in the horse's back the saddle will only be in contact with the body at two points – behind the withers and in front of the loins. The area of the back which usually supports most of the rider's weight will dip away under the saddle, putting extreme pressure on the two remaining points of contact. To remedy this the saddle must be carefully padded and supported from underneath.

When schooling a horse, one of the chief aims is to persuade him to lift and round his back, which enables the hind legs to be placed further underneath the body. This shifts the horse's centre of gravity back towards the quarters, enabling the weight of both horse and rider to be carried more by the quarters than the forehand. A sway-backed horse will obviously find this difficult to accomplish and will need a lot of help from a knowledgeable rider.

A roach back is one that rounds upwards over the loins, just before the croup. This conformation, although strong, gives problems because the saddle will be continually pushed forward, putting the rider out of balance. The horse's stride may also be jarring and uncomfortable for the rider.

Good conformation

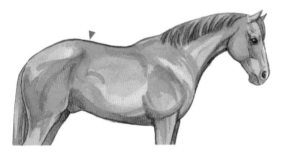

Roach back

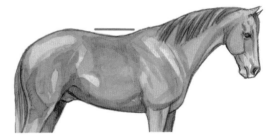

Short back

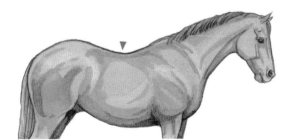

Dipped back

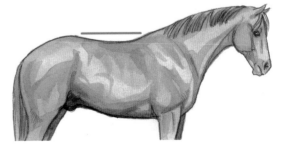

Long back

The Shoulders

Long sloping shoulders' are always mentioned with approval whenever the conformation of this region of the body is being discussed. This actually refers to the length of the scapula – or shoulder blade – and the angle at which it is set. Running along the middle of the scapula is a bony ridge which can normally be felt or seen, unless the horse is very fat. This ridge is used to assess the angle of the shoulder.

A line drawn along the scapular ridge should meet a line drawn horizontally through the body at an angle of approximately 45° - this is the ideal, and such a shoulder is termed 'well laid back'. An upright shoulder is one where the scapular ridge makes an angle which is greater than 45°.

A correctly angled scapula will be very efficient at absorbing the effects of concussion; it will also allow for freedom of movement and extension in the forelimb, giving a comfortable and athletic ride. A long scapula is advantageous because it gives plenty of room for muscle attachment.

If a horse has an upright shoulder he will be short-striding and limited in scope, finding extended paces difficult to achieve. He may also be more likely to suffer the effects of concussion on his legs and feet.

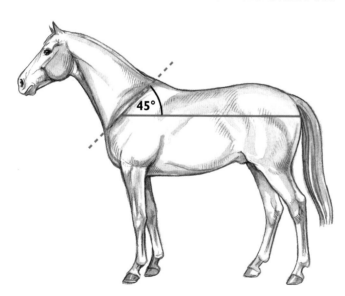

Correct, sloping shoulders - the angle between the scapular ridge and a line drawn horizontally through the body is 45°.

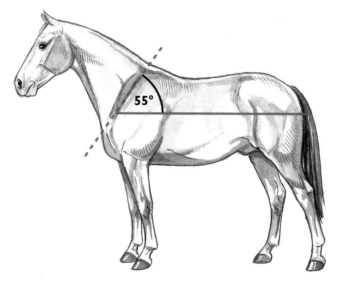

Upright shoulders. The angle between the scapular ridge and a line drawn horizonally through the body is greater than 45°.

THE ANATOMY OF:
(a) a correctly angled shoulder;
(b) an upright shoulder.

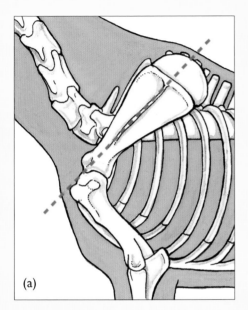

(a)

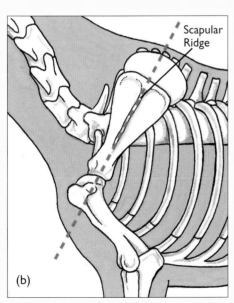

Scapular Ridge

(b)

In the case of loaded shoulders – often seen in combination with an upright scapula and low withers – the shoulder-blades are heavily covered with bulky muscle. The freedom and scope of the shoulders and forelimbs are restricted and the horse will move with a rolling gait. In addition to this, the width and bulk of the shoulder makes saddle-fitting very difficult as the saddle is continually being pushed backwards.

CROSS-SECTION THROUGH THE WITHER TO SHOW THE ANATOMY OF:
(a) a normal shoulder;
(b) a loaded shoulder.

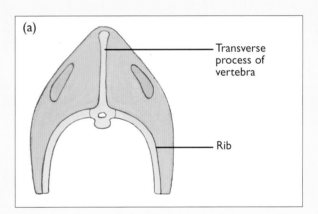

(a)

Transverse process of vertebra

Rib

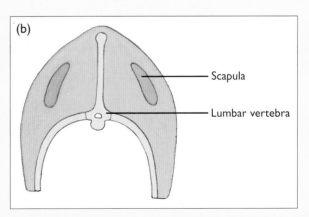

(b)

Scapula

Lumbar vertebra

A tied-in elbow – where the elbow joint is set too close to the ribcage – is also less than desirable, as lack of space in this area limits the movement of the shoulders and forelimbs. A horse with a tied-in elbow will have no freedom of movement; he will find lengthening his stride difficult and extension impossible.

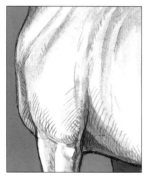

Correctly-placed elbow

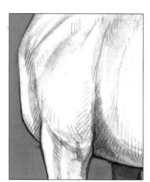

Tied-in elbow

THE ANATOMY OF THE SHOULDER FROM THE FRONT.

The shoulder and forelegs are connected to the ribcage and spine by soft tissue; there is no bony connection.

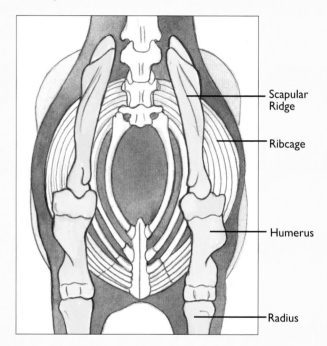

Scapular Ridge

Ribcage

Humerus

Radius

Upright shoulder limits movement

Sloping shoulder

The Hind Quarters

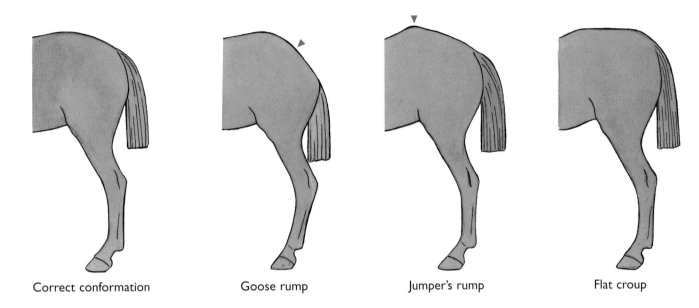

Correct conformation   Goose rump   Jumper's rump   Flat croup

The hind quarters should be strong, well-rounded and muscular. The horse's forward and upward movement originates from the powerful muscles located in the hind quarters. In order to provide maximum space for the attachment of these muscles, the framework (skeleton) of the hind quarters should be generous in all directions – length, width and depth. From behind, the hind quarters should appear to fit into a square (see fig. 2, page 8), from the side they should be rounded and flow in a gentle curve from the point of the croup to the base of the tail. If the quarters are flat between croup and tail, the horse may find it difficult to lower his hind quarters and engage his hind legs because of the angulation of his pelvis.

Quarters which slope steeply from croup to tail – known as 'goose rump' – have poor muscle structure and will therefore be weak, especially when coupled with bad hock conformation – as is often the case.

The so-called 'jumper's bump' is a noticeably sharp angle at the horse's croup caused by over development of the bones which form the point of croup. Many people believe this to be an advantage for a jumping horse as the bump provides extra space for muscle attachment – but this has never been proved. A jumper's bump coupled with good hind quarters and hock conformation should not be considered a fault.

The Hind Legs

Correct conformation

Camped out

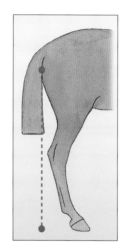

Camped under

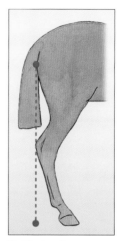

Sickle hocks

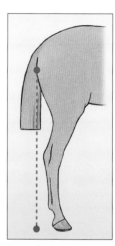

Straight leg

Seen from behind, the hind legs should appear to follow a straight line dropped vertically from the point of hip through the hock, cannon bone, fetlock and foot. Although the hock is usually positioned very slightly to the inside with the toe pointing slightly outwards – which is normal and correct – the cannon bone must always be vertical. If the hind leg does not conform to this principle, the structure as a whole will be weakened. Extra stress will be put on joints, or on a particular area of a joint, which may eventually result in damage.

If the hocks are angled inwards and the foot points outwards to the extent that the cannons slope away from the vertical – known as 'cow hocks' – stress will be placed on the outside of the hock and extra pressure will be put on the inner wall of the hoof. A horse with this conformation will not be able to carry a great deal of weight, but is usually able to stand up to moderate work.

In the case of a bow-legged horse – where the hock is angled outwards – extra pressure will be put on the inside of the hock whilst the outside ligaments will be stretched and weakened. The outer wall of the hoof will receive greater pressure than the inner wall, which will affect the wear of the horn. Seen from the side, a vertical line dropped from the point of buttock should almost touch the hock, then run parallel and almost touching the cannon bone. If the foot is positioned to the outside of the vertical the horse is said to be 'camped-out'. This

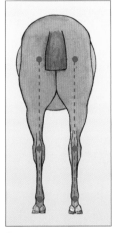
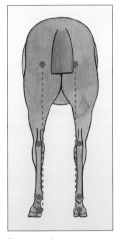
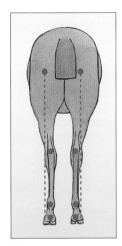
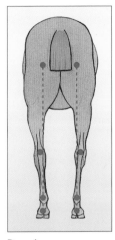
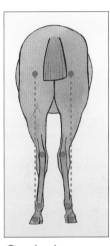

| Correct | Base wide | Base narrow | Bow legs | Cow hocks |

conformation puts strain not only on the hock but also on the muscles of the back and loins. The horse will also have difficulty engaging the hind legs.

If the leg is angled inside the vertical – termed 'under itself behind' – again there is strain on the hock and a greater possibility of forging (the hoof of the hind leg striking against the sole of the forefoot on the same side).

If the angle of the leg at the hock is too acute – 'sickle hocks' – stress is placed on the whole structure of the hock joint, and also on the ligaments nd tendons which support the fetlock and foot. This conformation is very weak; the horse will have little pushing power from behind and the structure as a whole would not stand up to hard,

prolonged work in any discipline. A horse with this conformation is often referred to as having 'curby hocks'. A curb is a swelling which appears about four inches below the point of the hock, as the result of damage to the ligament which connects the tarsus – or hock – to the cannon bone at the back of the leg.

In severe cases the swelling becomes hard and bony, and can affect the soundness of the horse.

In an over-straight leg the cannon bone will be vertical, but will be positioned in front of the vertical line from the point of buttock to the ground. The hock, fetlock and pasterns will all be straight giving the leg a stiff-like appearance. The whole structure of the leg will be stressed by the inability of the upright joints to absorb concussion. A straight leg has less spring than one which is correctly angled, so the stride will not be rounded and flowing. Jumping ability will also be reduced.

Other factors of good hind leg conformation are:

• The hock should be 'well let down' – meaning that there should be plenty of length from the hip to the hock.
• The cannon bones should be short and strong.
• The hock and fetlock joints should be hard, flat and clean, free from any heat, lumps or swellings.
• The second thigh should be well muscled.

FAULTS IN THE HIND LEG

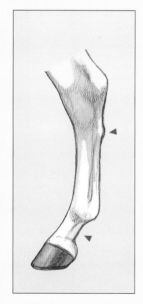

Curb, and weak, sloping pasterns

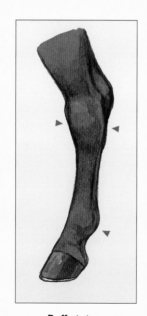

Puffy joints

Sickle hock

Long cannon bones, upright pasterns

Looking at the Differences

Although the basic structures of every horse's body must conform to the same principles if he is to stay sound, considerable variation in shape, size and proportion can be seen in the physical make-up of the different breeds and types. These differences came about in two ways : the first being the process of evolution and natural selection, where the horse's body was shaped by the need to survive in its environment ; the second being the rather unnatural selection imposed upon the horse by man in order to fulfil his own needs.

Exmoor

Before domestication, the shape of the horse was dictated entirely by the need to survive in its own particular habitat. Those horses who lived in a cold climate evolved physical characteristics which minimised heat loss, and are known as 'cold-blooded.' This does not refer to the actual body temperature - which is the same in all horses - but rather to their mental and physical make-up. All cold-bloods - such as cobs, heavy horses and hairy ponies - have physical similarities which can be traced back to the process of natural selection by the extremes of a cold, wet climate.

• The shape of the body is round and stocky. Less heat is lost by a short, thick object than by a long, thin one of the same weight, because the thicker object has less surface area (thick, chunky chips take much longer to cool down than French fries, for example); the neck is short and thick for the same reason.

• The legs are short, which limits the circulation of air round the barrel.
• The skin is thick and well provided with insulating fat cells.
• The hair of the coat is thick, coarse and long, allowing an insulating layer of air to be trapped around the body.
• The thick coat also serves as a waterproof layer, which protects the body from rain and snow.
• Long hair, or ' feather, ' grows on the lower leg and heels, preventing heat loss and protecting the skin from damage by mud or water.
• The mane and forelock are long and thick, protecting the neck and head from both cold and rain.
• The tail is bushy and long; it is usually set low down on the quarters to protect the thin skin of the inner thighs.
• The shape of the nose is often convex due to the large, underlying nasal air-passages that warm the inhaled air before it reaches the lungs.
• The nostrils are small, and close easily.
• The jaws are large to accommodate the heavy-duty teeth necessary to a horse grazing on tough vegetation.
• The movement of a cold-blooded horse is often slow, and he usually has a calm and equable temperament to match.

The Exmoor pony is an example of an animal that has adapted to live in cold, harsh conditions. It is thought to be directly descended from ponies of pre-historic times due to the inaccessibility of its moor-land habitat; it possesses many of the

Caspian

The tail hair is fine, and the tail itself is usually carried away from the body when the horse moves.
• The skin is thin, which enables the veins to stand out on its surface in order to cool the blood.
• The skin is well supplied with sweat glands, the evaporation of sweat being an efficient way of lowering body temperature.
• The shape of the head is light and refined, as the desert horse does not need the heavy teeth or the large nasal air-passages of the cold-blood.
• The nostrils are large and open.
• This horse is fast and agile; he is also hot-blooded by nature, being sensitive, fiery and quick to react.

characteristics listed above. In order to survive the extreme climate of Exmoor, the pony has evolved a particularly effective coat consisting of an insulating , woolly under-layer covered by long, greasy hair which completely repels water. So efficient is this coat at preventing heat loss from the body that the pony can walk round for days covered in a layer of snow.

By contrast, the body of a horse that evolved in hot, desert conditions (known as a 'hot-blood') has become adapted to lose heat as quickly and efficiently as possible.
• The barrel and neck are longer and leaner (the French-fry, as opposed to the chunky chip!)
• The legs are longer to allow maximum circulation of air around the body.
• The coat is fine and silky and the legs lack feather.
• The mane is fine, but still long enough to give protection from the sun and flies.

The Caspian is another direct descendent from the horses of pre-history, but as his ancestors lived in the deserts of Central Asia, he has evolved many of the characteristics necessary for survival in these conditions. Although he is referred to as a pony (he stands 10-12 hh), the Caspian is, in fact, a miniature horse, having both the proportions and characteristics of a horse rather than those of a pony. He is one of the oldest, living equine breeds - only the Asiatic Wild Horse is known to be older. It is thought that the Caspian shares the same ancestry as the Arab horse.

Heavy Horse - Percheron

The conformation of these two horses could not be more different, but the body of each has become perfectly adapted to the job it has to do. The heavy horse needs strength, but not speed - a need which is reflected in every part of his anatomy.

• The hind quarters are large and muscular; they are the source of the heavy horse's immense power.

• The back is short - again to give strength - and the loins are wide.

• The croup is often prominent and the quarters slightly sloping to allow the horse to engage his hocks well under his body for maximum pushing power.

• The conformation of the withers and shoulders differs from that of a ridden horse; the withers are flatter whilst the shoulders are more upright to enable the horse to push his weight into the harness without discomfort.

• The legs are short, with plenty of hard, solid bone. The cannons should be short, and the joints large and flat.

• The pasterns are short and strong rather than long and sloping.

• The chest is broad and deep, with plenty of room for heart and lungs.

• The neck is short and powerful.

When horses were first domesticated and used by humans for their own needs, the hitherto slow process of change began to gather momentum. From a few original primitive types man has created a multitude of horses and ponies of every shape, size and function. The two extremes of this process of selective breeding are, on the one hand, the heavy horse - designed for hard, slow, heavy work - and on the other, the English Thoroughbred - designed for the sole purpose of getting from one place to another as quickly as possible.

The Percheron originated in Normandy; he is immensely strong, and rather elegant for a heavy horse - due to the input of Barb and Arab blood way back in his ancestry. A pure-bred Percheron holds the unofficial pulling record of 1547 kg (3410 pounds); Percherons have also been used in war, in agriculture and under harness. Most of the characteristics of the cold-blood can be seen in this horse; the addition of oriental blood has refined his head and given him better action than most other heavy breeds.

The body of the Thoroughbred has been adapted for speed and not for strength. Every inch of his body is streamlined, every bone is sharp and sculpted, every muscle is taut and toned.
• The body is long and lean.
• The withers are well defined and the shoulders are long and sloping - this gives the thoroughbred his long, low gallop.
• The neck is long, lean and well shaped to help with balance.
• The girth is deep and the chest is spacious to give plenty of room for heart and lungs.
• The legs are long - occasionally the length of the hind leg in a sprinter results in croup-high conformation.
• The hocks are strong and well-formed to give maximum propulsion.
• The quarters are large and well-muscled; the loins are wide, short and muscular.
• The pasterns are long and sloping.
• The head is small and refined.

The Thoroughbred was developed in 17th and 18th century England, specifically for racing. Fast native horses and ponies were crossed with imported Arabians to produce a horse with superb speed, stamina and courage - an animal that has had more influence on the breeding of horses than any other.

The Thoroughbred is not a 'pure' hot-blood, due to the early influence of native blood; neither is the Percheron purely cold-blooded due to his share of Arabian genes. In both these horses man has taken the raw material offered by nature and developed the qualities of each to perfection.

Thoroughbred

Breeds

These are breeds of horses and ponies which have been developed by man over many generations, each for a particular purpose. Every horse has a different conformation, as every horse has a different job to do.

Lipizzaner - (15.1 - 16.1 hh)

This is a horse used at the Spanish Riding School of Vienna; he is descended from an old breed of Spanish Horse imported to Vienna in the 16th century. He is bred to perform Classical Equitation – also known as 'High School'. This discipline has movements which demand the ultimate degree of collection, consequently the Lipizzaner is built for strength and not for speed. He is short and compact, with a strongly muscled neck and powerful hind quarters. His neck is set high on the shoulder, which makes collection easy to achieve. He occasionally has the convex Roman nose of his Spanish forebears.

The Hackney Horse – (15 - 15.3 hh)

This horse was bred to be an elegant carriage horse with very extravagant paces. His neck is long and well-shaped, rising almost vertically out of his shoulder. His head is always carried high – as is his tail. As a carriage horse his wither is not well-defined, but his shoulders are powerful. His head is small and neat, with a convex profile. The feet are allowed to grow long to encourage him to lift his legs sharply off the ground. His flamboyant paces are mainly inherited from his ancestors – the English trotting horses of the eighteenth century.

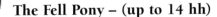

The Fell Pony – (up to 14 hh)

It is thought that the Fell is partly descended from the black Friesian horses brought over to Northern Europe by the Roman cavalry. The Fell began as an all-purpose animal – pulling a trap, carrying panniers and able to take a full-grown man for a day's shepherding or hunting. His shape is not ideal for a riding pony as his withers are very flat. The general impression is one of great strength. The abundant tail is carried low, and the heels have much feathering. As he is expected to be capable of crossing any kind of country his action is rounded, with lift at the knee.

The American Quarter Horse – (14.3 - 16 hh)

The Quarter Horse was developed in colonial America from horses imported from England crossed with the local stock of Spanish origin. The settlers used them for sprint racing over distances of a quarter of a mile – hence the name ; and also as cow ponies and for lighter harness work. The quarters are deep, wide and exceptionally well-muscled. His back is short and close-coupled; with long, well-defined withers which give good anchorage to the saddle.

49

Types

These are 'types' of horses and ponies. A type is not a breed, but rather a category into which a horse can be fitted – often for showing purposes.

The Cob – (show limit 15.1 hh)

The Cob originated as a utility horse. He would have been put to harness, done a day's hunting and could also be used for every-day riding. His temperament should be calm, his build strong, sturdy and close-coupled ; his back and legs short and his hind quarters round and muscular. His neck is short, well shaped and crested, with the mane hogged for showing. His movement should be low but he should have the ability to gallop. Welsh Cobs and Norman Cobs are breeds, but the ordinary Cob is of no fixed parentage – some are pure Irish Draught, others may be of Shire, Cleveland or Welsh Cob descent.

The Riding Pony – (up to 14.2 hh)

The Riding Pony is a triumph of selective breeding - being in a effect a miniature version of the Thoroughbred Horse whilst still retaining the type, substance and character of his native pony ancestors. Thoroughbred and Arab blood was mixed with that of Dartmoor and Welsh Ponies to arrive at the finished product, which was developed purely for the show ring. His conformation should not only be faultless, it should also cater to the needs of his juvenile rider – his body should be narrow enough for the child to sit comfortably and his neck should not be so thick and powerful that the child would lack control.

The Hack – (14.2 - 15.3 hh)

Now only seen in the show ring, the Hack is a purely British type. It evolved in the days when the fashionable elite rode out in Hyde Park's Rotten Row in order to show off their outfits, horse and horsemanship. Elegance, lightness, good manners and impeccable schooling are the qualities necessary to the successful Hack. Basic good conformation is fundamental ; most Hacks are pure thoroughbred, but the small Hack will have the addition of some Arab or pony blood. The action is low, smooth and graceful; at the trot the toe should be pointed and there should be no excessive lifting of the knee.

The Hunter - (height variable)

This is a horse who must carry his rider for hours across country ; he must be sound in every respect, and correct structural conformation is a necessity. The type of horse varies with the type of country to be ridden through ; on good pasture a near-thoroughbred with a good gallop is ideal, whereas on hills or plough a horse with more power and shorter legs will be needed. The show hunter needs to combine both quality and substance with a deep girth, a back of medium length, powerful quarters, strong limbs and correct feet. The Irish Draught, Cleveland Bay and many native pony breeds will make excellent hunters when crossed with a thoroughbred.

Choosing the Right Horse for the Job

Each discipline (dressage, show jumping, eventing, distance riding, etc.) makes different demands on its equine participants, and each puts its own stress on varying parts of the horse's body. Although the majority of horses and ponies will be able to participate in most disciplines at riding club level, when selecting a horse or pony to compete at advanced levels it is crucial to choose an animal whose conformation will help rather than hinder his progress.

Temperament plays a very important part in the success of any horse performing at any level in any discipline. A horse being made to work in a way that his body cannot support will be in constant discomfort; as a result he will eventually become short-tempered and uncooperative. For both your own and the horse's benefit it is well worthwhile examining what demands are to be made on the horse by the chosen discipline, and which physical characteristics are best able to fulfil them.

Dressage

'Dressage' is just another word for schooling or training. Every ridden horse, no matter which discipline he will take up in later life, will begin his career with a period of dressage training. This preliminary schooling is designed to familiarise the horse with such necessary procedures as stopping and starting, steering and transitions through the paces. In order for the young horse to be able to carry the extra weight of a rider his muscles must be developed and strengthened; again this is part and parcel of his basic training.

In the more specialised use of the term, dressage refers to the branch of equestrian competitive sport where schooling becomes an end in itself. At the lowest levels, dressage tests ask no more from the horse than the ability to walk, trot, canter and halt when and where required, and to execute not-too-demanding figures obediently and in natural balance. To compete at this level is within the scope of every sound horse and pony: even those with less than fortunate conformation. What is being judged is the correctness of the horse's basic training, along with his obedience, relaxation and calmness. A horse with only average conformation but a good, calm temperament will have a distinct advantage over a horse with excellent paces and conformation but a mind of his own.

As the tests become more difficult, conformation plays an increasing role in the horse's ability to perform and achieve. One of the basic aims of dressage schooling is to teach the horse to collect. Collection is the shortening and rounding of the frame brought about by training the horse to lift his neck and back, lower the hindquarters and engage the hind legs (bringing them further

A good type of dressage horse.

(1) A young horse at the early stage of training. The weight is on the forehand.

(2) Intermediate stage. The weight is more evenly balanced.

(3) Advanced stage. The weight is carried by the quarters.

underneath his body). As a result of collection the horse's steps become shorter and higher but without any slowing or quickening of his rhythm. The horse begins to transfer his weight and that of his rider from the forehand to the quarters; this improves his lightness, power and agility.

As you can see in fig. 1 the way of going for a horse at Preliminary level (the first stage of training) involves no more than working in natural balance and moving freely forward in a slightly rounded outline. Again, most horses will find no problem working at this level, but those with conformational defects which affect the ability to stretch the neck and accept the bit – such as ewe neck, swan neck and a thick neck coupled with heavy jaws - will already be starting to struggle. A moderately low-set head and neck will be an advantage in competitions at this level, where the required outline is long and low.

A horse at the intermediate stage of training (fig. 2) is showing a greater degree of engagement and collection, which will be beyond the ability of those horses with faulty back conformation (exit those with sway backs, roach backs, or those who are croup high).

The horse in fig. 3 is working at advanced level, in maximum collection, with lowered hindquarters and corresponding elevation of the forehand. The hindquarters are now bearing an increased proportion of weight; in order to bring the hind leg under the body the horse must compress all three joints of the quarters (hip, stifle and hock) and lower his pelvis from the sacro-iliac. Good, strong conformation of this region of the body is vital – so here we will lose those with weak quarters, weak loins, goose rumps, flat croups, long backs, sickle hocks and straight hind legs. At this stage of training a naturally high head and neck carriage will be an advantage.

The rounded and elevated paces of a dressage horse at extended trot.

When assessing a horse for a future in dressage, the most important factor to consider is his movement. He should be supple and flexible in every joint: flexion in the hock being particularly relevant, as this will give elevation to the paces and also enable passage and piaffe to be developed at a later stage in his training.

The horse will be judged on the correctness of his paces, so good gaits – in dressage terms – are vital. At walk, the steps should be long and free-striding, with the hind feet overtracking the forefeet. The trot should be rounded and active, with the horse using both fore and hind legs equally. Low action, with the feet flicking out at the end of the stride, is not so desirable. The canter should also be active and round, with the hind legs engaged well underneath the body. If the horse lifts well off the ground in trot and canter he will not have difficulty working in collection; it is easier to train a horse to lengthen than to shorten his stride.

The majority of horses working at top level in dressage today are warmbloods of one type or another – a warmblood being any horse with a mixture of thoroughbred (hot blood) and heavy horse (cold blood) in its breeding. Pure thoroughbreds are occasionally seen competing at top level, but their conformation, paces and temperament are not ideally suited to dressage. They have been selectively bred for generations to gallop, whereas the modern competition warmblood has been carefully developed to have the appropriate physical and mental attributes to excel at dressage.

Show Jumping

A good type of show jumper

In contrast to the successful dressage horse, who conforms to a fairly limited range of type and breeding, the shape and size of the top-class show jumper can be far more varied. Looks, type and height are not relevant to jumping ability; what is important is that the conformation of the horse is well balanced – that the hind quarters and forehand match each other in size and power.

The conformation of the hindquarters and hind legs should be strong and correct, as the horse's power to lift himself and his rider off the ground comes from the muscles in ths part of the body. Any conformation defect in this area – such as weak loins, a goose-rump, trailing hocks, sickle hocks or weak sloping pasterns should be avoided in a horse intended to compete at higher levels. Considerable stress is also placed on the horse's forehand and forelegs when the horse lands after jumping; good conformation here will help absorb the resulting impact and concussion. Faulty foot and pastern conformation would be likely to sustain damage, as would a leg which is back at the knee. Correct shoulder conformation will help to reduce damage from concussion, and also enable the horse to lift his forehand on take-off. Well-shaped withers, back and barrel will all help to ensure that saddle and rider stay in correct balance during the many shifts of weight and position involved in jumping a fence. As the head and neck play such an important role in balancing the horse over a jump, good conformation in these areas is vital. A short neck or a large head will adversely affect the horse's ability to balance himself, both over the jump and on landing and recovery.

Unlike the dressage horse, a show jumper does not need to possess exceptional pace. In the confines of the show jumping arena an extravagant canter can be difficult to control, as can the free paces of the event horse; a short-striding horse can lack the scope necessary to jump big courses. For this discipline a horse with naturally well balanced, middle-of-the-range paces will be the one to choose.

Temperament is an important factor to consider in a show jumper. A combination of sharpness and obedience is ideal – the horse should want to forwards into the jump without hotting up to such an extent that he fights his rider. Although temperament is not governed by conformation, the horse whose body is well-constructed for jumping will be more obliging than one who is in pain or discomfort from being made to do a job for which he was not designed.

The correct outline for a horse jumping a fence. His body makes a graceful curve - or 'bascule' - from back to front; this enables maximum use of energy.

The horse is jumping flat. His back is hollow and his head and neck are lifted; this is a very inefficient use of energy.

Eventing

A good type of event horse.

Although many unremarkable horses compete successfully at local and novice one-day events, to succeed in top-class eventing the horse must be an outstanding all-round athlete. The standard of dressage and show jumping required from the event horse may not be so high as that needed by a pure dressage or show jumping horse, but he must still perform with considerable efficiency. The level of fitness and stamina necessary to compete at top-level eventing is certainly far higher than that required by the other disciplines; all this must be combined with the courage and ability to jump a variety of fearsomely imposing obstacles.

Most of the horses competing in three-day eventing are either pure thoroughbred (of the more solid point-to-pointer type rather than the lighter type bred for flat racing) or near-thoroughbred crosses. Horse's without a high percentage of thoroughbred blood will not have the ability to gallop at the speed necessary to complete the cross-country in the optimum time. The addition of a small amount of heavy-horse blood (often Irish draught) adds the substance and bone which can be lacking in the thoroughbred.

The ideal conformation for an event horse is very similar to that for the point-to-pointer. Soundness is extremely important, as eventing is a very difficult and testing sport. The training involved in getting the horse fit and competent enough to compete is demanding and rigorous in itself, and will bring to light any weaknesses in conformation. The limbs in particular must be strong, sound and free from any defects. The pasterns should be correctly angled; upright pasterns will not absorb the effects of concussion, and sloping pasterns will be too weak to withstand the stresses of galloping and jumping. The hocks should be strong and well-made; weak or sickle hocks are very likely to break down, and should be avoided at all costs. The tendons of the leg should be clean and hard, with no signs of damage.

The event horse needs to have a good, ground-covering gallop.

Any fault which will limit the horse's ability to gallop freely – such as straight hind legs, upright shoulders, an over-short neck or back – should also be avoided. The chest and barrel should be wide and deep enough to accommodate the good set of heart and lungs so necessary for strength and stamina.

The stride of the eventer should be long, free and swinging. He is not required to show collection, as is the dressage horse, and neither does he need to jump with the same degree of bascule as the show jumper – but he does need to be able to cover the ground at a good, active gallop.

Temperament is again very important in the event horse. He needs to be calm enough to perform a dressage test when at the very peak of fitness; bold enough to jump the demanding cross-country course; and yet still have the obedience required to complete a round of show jumps…superhorse, indeed!

Endurance Riding

A good type of horse for endurance riding.

Endurance – or long-distance – riding used to be thought of as the last resort for the horse and rider who lacked the ability to compete at dressage and the nerve to showjump or event.

This is far from the case today; endurance riding is now the fastest growing discipline in the equestrian world.

The distance to be covered varies from 40km (25 miles) covered at 8 km/h (5 mph) to 160 km (100 miles) to be completed in two days. To compete at even the lowest level the horse must be strong in every structure and function – but particularly important are the limbs, feet, heart and lungs, as these are the parts of the body which receive the most stress and pressure. Good conformation is therefore essential for this horse; his balance and symmetry should be correct, he should have straight limbs, hard hooves, a deep chest and powerful quarters. His back should be short-coupled for strength; a long back and slack loins will be too weak to withstand this amount of work. The ideal height for the endurance horse is between 14.3 and 15.3hh; he needs a good ground-covering stride and paces which are comfortable and smooth.

Most of today's successful endurance horses are either Arabs or Arab crosses, as this breed possesses most of the physical attributes necessary for the job – strong bones, hard feet, endless stamina and a short, strong back. (The Arab has 17 ribs, 5 lumbar vertebrae and 16 caudal vertebrae, whereas other horses have 18, 6, 18 respectively).

The Best Friend

The 'best-friend' is the type of horse or pony that many of us end up with: not a top-class performance horse, but a good all-rounder who can take part in most disciplines at riding-club level, or maybe just hack happily around the countryside. The stresses and strains on the structure of an all-rounder are far less than those experienced by a horse competing regularly at a high level, therefore one can be more forgiving when assessing his conformation.

Any outstandingly obvious defect in the structure of the horse's body should give cause for concern: for instance, an excessively long back, or very long sloping pasterns could give problems to an animal doing even a moderate amount of work. Any noticeable asymmetry – such as misalignment of the cannon and pastern bones, or displacement of the pelvis – could lead to unsoundness and are best avoided. Poorly-shaped hocks, and sickle hocks in particular, are weak and will not stand up to consistent work; neither will feet with bad conformation.

Minor defects in conformation need not rule out a horse for all-round use. A horse with a flat croup may have difficulty mastering piaffe and passage, but unless your sights are set on competing at Grand Prix level this need not inconvenience either of you!

If you are now looking with a jaundiced eye at your best-friend of many years standing – i.e. noticing his various deficiencies for the first time and wondering if maybe you should stop jumping him at local shows out of consideration for his upright pasterns and straight hind leg – please don't! If a horse is performing well and willingly he is unlikely to be in any great physical discomfort. However, when planning his schedule, you must take his conformational deficiencies into account. Try to keep his work-schedule within safe limits, to avoid over-stressing the weak links in his anatomy.

Being aware of your horse's faults will enable you to monitor his condition. If his leg conformation is less than ideal you should check regularly for any heat, lumps or swellings which would indicate the beginning of a problem, and adjust his work accordingly.

Above all, listen to your horse. He may be trying to tell you that he is not comfortable in the only way he can – by being uncooperative. Physical discomfort, rather than naughtiness, can be the cause of much of the horse's bad behaviour. Knowing the principles of good conformation (and understanding the problems resulting from bad conformation) will lead not only to greater harmony between you and your horse, but will also help to prolong your happy and healthy partnership.

Index